2015

NAMESAKE

Also by Joan Fiset

Now the Day is Over

NAMESAKE

Joan Fiset

*for Maureen &
with deepest
thanks
Joan
November
2015*

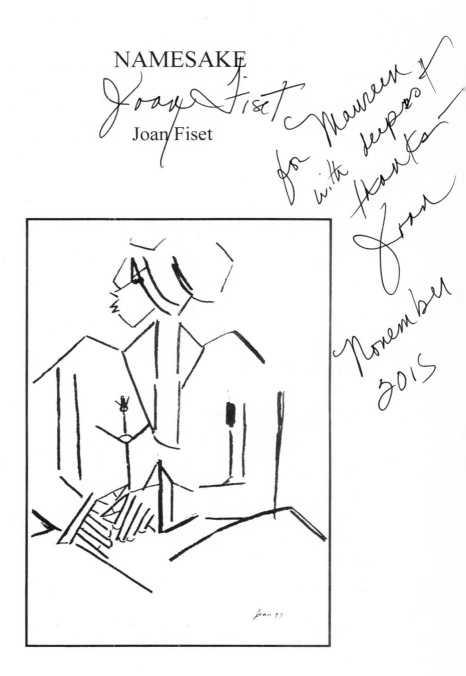

Blue Begonia Press Selah, Washington

Acknowledgments

Thanks to Elana Zaiman, Ann Eisenberg, Marcia Robbins, Bodeen, Jeff Eaton, Susan Bradford, Louis Fiset ~

Five Blocks to Green Lake Photograph by Gary Grenell
Title page: India Ink Sketch by Joan Bradford, The Multimedia Work of Joan Bradford, Sargent Gallery, Sewanee, Tennessee, September 1 – 30, 1997

ISBN: 978-0-911287-74-5

Cover design by Amy Peters
Author photo by Louis Fiset

Blue Begonia Press
311 Hillcrest Drive Selah, WA
bluebegoniapress.com

for Louis, and for our family

Goodnight room
Goodnight moon
Goodnight cow
jumping over the moon
Goodnight light
And the red balloon

Contents

III *when it falls over water*

VI   *no more reaching*

Namesake

My mother was named after Joan of Arc. I am named after my mother. She used to tell me stories of the peasant girl who never learned to read. When she milked the cows she heard voices telling her to save France. She wore a suit of armor when she rode on horseback holding the French flag high as she led the soldiers into war. My mother said she was burned at the stake. I used to imagine her tied to a wooden pole while tongues of fire licked her ankles then moved upward until the red flames and smoke consumed her. I envisioned her looking up to the sky, as if somehow she understood this horrible thing happening to her. When my mother said Joan of Arc was born to save her country her voice grew serious and calm. She said she became Saint Joan because of her suffering. She talked about Joan of Arc as if we were she and she was us.

I

into early the water blue overhead a capable sky
sag of hem no scatter or singe as yet in view

Joan Stone 12 years-old
Franklin, Pennsylvania 1929

Performance

In the Seminary where my father is a divinity student someone plays a piano. My father says to my mother, "Sing, 'Just Plain Bill.'" She stands next to the piano and smiles, tilts her head to the side and begins to sing, "He's just a simple, guy, my Bill . . ." Her voice clear like water rippling. Then "Sentimental Journey." When she sings, "Got my bags, got my reservation. Spent each dime I could afford. Like a child in wild anticipation, I long to hear that 'all l l l l- aboard,'" I don't understand what all the words mean, but can tell she's going somewhere with a suitcase in her hand. Everyone joins in when she sings, "Seven . . . that's the time we leave at seven, I'll be waitin' up for heaven, countin' every mile of railroad track that takes me back . . ." I see her leaving, but not in a song.

Reflection

I am four. We look into the mirror above the dresser. My mother's
brow is furrowed. I notice straight lines and say, "Your forehead looks
like a flag."

Potholes

In nursery school my hair grows snarls; lumpy wadded tangles
impossible to comb. My mother explains they come from my sleep.
Brushing my hair to cover them she tells me, "They're hiding now.
No one will ever guess."

When they grow too big my father cuts them out; scissors leave holes
I touch with my fingers.

"Don't worry," she would say. "Your hair always grows back, hair the
color of wheat just like the Little Prince."

Prized

When I say "waterwalls" instead of "overalls" she writes it down. She exclaims over "my dear little elbow." I believe I am adored like the child in the cabbage patch. My mother reads me this story again and again as I sit on her lap imagining shiny purple green leaves of the cabbage, the woman's patched apron as she leans down to pick up the treasured baby she's longed for and wants for her own.

Harm

Babar the Elephant is my first book. My mother reads it to me in our apartment in the Seminary. When we come to the green elephant who ate poisonous mushrooms I tell her to stop.

He's melting into wrinkles. Cannot stand up. "This is a calamity," my mother says.

I know the elephant is going to die.

Lullaby

Every month a record arrives from the Children's Record Club.
Chorus of deep voices, "We're building a city, we're building a city,
here is for the postman, here is for the fireman, we're building a city
today." The record jacket shows small stocky men running around
with saws and hammers against a red background.

On the record of *Tubby the Tuba* mournful music, tuba low like it can't
stand up straight, underwater reaching toward the air.

My favorite record is the family where the crying baby can't sleep
until the mother sings about the pigeon house:

> *My pigeon house I open wide,*
> *And set my pigeons free.*
> *They fly so high till they reach the sky*
> *to light on the tallest tree.*
>
> *And when they return to their merry merry nest,*
> *I shut the door and I say goodnight,*
> *coo-roo,coo-roo, coo-roo, coo-roo,*
> *coo roo, coo-roo, coo-roo.*

My mother sings "My Pigeon House" every night until I fall asleep.

Open House

In first grade I draw a house with a yellow thatched roof and blue
Dutch door open halfway up. Curtains tied back at the window, white
with green polka dots; flowers bloom in front, their petals red, purple,
and orange on green stalks with leaves.

At Parents' Open House we stand beside our desks. The classroom
overflows with mothers and fathers. In the doorway my mother, just
outside leaning in, eyes open wide. I see her smiling down at me, the
folder of my work open for inspection, picture of the house on top.

Power

We're coloring outside. It's summer, crayons spread out every which way on the table. We both draw horses. I attempt a brown and white pinto's mane, forelock, sloped head, brown eyes. "Mine's better," I announce to my mother who does not disagree, who looks down and keeps sketching as if she knows she'll never come close to the perfect horse I claim is mine.

Summit

Wearing a red gingham-check maternity top my mother plays
"The Big Rock Candy Mountain" on our upright piano, sings:

> *lemonade springs*
> *where the bluebird sings*
> *on the big rock candy mountain . . .*

Her hands a blur up and down the keys. I imagine a mountain,
sugar jagged as ice.

Letter from My Mother   March 15, 1988

Grace Ray.

In the tender years of my beginning I knew her.

*I was seven when I entered her house to study piano. Once a week
I sat on her swivel stool to read the large black notes before me.
"Oh where, oh where has my little dog gone?" My hands were
small and eager.*

*I can still see her solemn sallow face, her grey perfect hair marcels.
Music in her she instilled in me. An hour a day I practiced for many
years. My grandmother secluded in the pantry making cookies listened
sustaining me. The Stein lamp flooding my pages of music till my
fingers flew in ecstasy commanding the broad keyboard of black and
white. The talent was in me. These teachers drew it out, watered it
with praise. The feeling was deep that I had pulled from my agile
fingers. How tenderly I remember these two piano teachers, their
patience that guided me like beacons. I still smell the quaint summer
roses drifting through the window, smell the slow cooking in Mrs.
Kesseman's homey kitchen as she moved through the door holding her
stirring spoon high instructing me, her rumpled hair, untidily falling
about her gentle face (her young son drowned in the nearby Allegheny
river one snowy night when his sled failed to stop) I remember how
she said my gift at the piano was great. I remember how filled I was
with happiness in my littleness.*

*Now tears mingle with the notes of music they bequeathed to me.
Many decades have passed, yet I miss these noble women and my
music lessons and the shiny leaves that grew from the rooted plant
that stood on Grace Ray's sturdy table by the large window in the
mysterious room, where melodies started in my nimble fingers grew
into Concertos of Love, Symphonies of Praise, fingers of Joy, Hymns
of Glory, Wells of Salvation, Rivers of Peace. One glorious Amen.*

Susan Elisabeth

I sit on the front stairs of our parsonage in Oxford. My father's home from Worcester where he drove my mother to have my new baby sister. He walks across the yard; dark slacks, white shirt. His face is glazed. My sister has *tiny hands and tiny tiny fingernails*. He smiles far away from where I'm listening.

I have a picture book, a boy with a new baby brother he holds in a pillow. I don't feel like a big sister, even though everyone says that's what I'm going to be.

When my mother and sister come home from the hospital Eleanor Walker who cleans our house takes care of our baby while my mother stays in bed. Mrs. Walker swabs something bright orange from a small brown bottle onto my sister's belly button. A big knot. She ties a wide belly-button band around it until it heals.

My sister turns her head from side to side, waves her hands. She kicks her feet in the air. On her wrist pink beads of a bracelet spell her name. Mrs. Walker leans close, "That's a good girl," swoops her up then down the hall in the crook of her arm.

Armed

We visit my mother and father's friends in a house with dark wooden walls. I'm six and wear a black velvet skirt with velvet straps crossed in back. Organdy puff-sleeved blouse. I climb upstairs while the others talk in the living room. Landing. Small alcove with a dresser against the wall. I open a drawer; see a gun. I pick it up. It's heavy. Holding it in both hands, finger tucked into the curve of the trigger, I walk out to the top of the stairs. Point the gun at my parents.

A woman runs up the stairs. She talks in a soft voice while she reaches out her hand. My mother looks startled and stiff. My father stops talking. His mouth is open. Everyone looks at me until the woman has slipped the gun out of my hands. I stand very still as she takes it away.

Shelter

Painted turtle at the dime store, shell orange with a red flower and green leaves. An orange paper parasol comes with him. I put him in a glass pie plate on the kitchen table with two rocks he can climb up on. Turtle food from a small can filled with flakes. They float on the water until he eats them. He raises his head, looks around. My mother says he carries his house on his back. His home always with him, he pulls in his feet, head, and tail. Then he's safe. No one can hurt him or take away his house. The orange parasol stands open on one of the rocks, toothpick handle stuck into green modeling clay I rolled between my hands.

Quicksand

My mother warns me not to go near the pond by Dottie French's house because it has quicksand, and I'll disappear. Cars, horses, cows slowly sink until the quicksand covers them. I want to be near it, look at the pond from behind a fence.

One morning I walk to Dottie French's house. There are five children in her family. Sometimes Dottie comes over to play. The French kids are scruffy; dirt on their faces, knotted broken shoelaces. Their parents never know where they are.

I spot the pond from behind the fence. Water reflects white clouds. As I lean against it I look over my shoulder. Far away my mother walks toward me in her navy blue car coat with a red and gray plaid flannel lining. I turn around, pretend I don't see her. She walks to where I stand. Hand on my shoulder, "Come home."

Part of my punishment is to stay in my room. It's Saturday. My father's having a Popcorn Party at the parsonage, and I always go. Today I sit on my bed listening to kids as they arrive. My mother brings lunch, sandwich with three slices of tomato on a plate. Later my father comes upstairs. He's going to spank me for going to the quicksand.

I run down the hall, lock myself in the bathroom. He tells me, "Open the door." When I finally unlock it he walks me back to the bedroom, turns me over his knee and says, "This is going to hurt me more than it's going to hurt you."

I should have stayed in the yard. Tree stump and pine needles where I pretend wooden clothespins are children.

Hideout

My mother and I stayed with my grandmother and grandfather in
the parsonage in Providence, Rhode Island while my father was in the
war. My mother tells me my grandmother told her she "hated babies."
She wouldn't let her feed me. I was on a schedule; she gave me a
bottle at certain times. I cried and cried. She told me this as long as
I can remember. I know the words before she says them and imagine
the baby at the end of the long hallway. Birds bring crumbs through
the window into a room dim like in the pantry off the kitchen where
I hide and no one finds me.

Houseguest

My father is Walter's Sponsor. He was in jail and is out on parole.
Walter comes to live with us for awhile. He and my mother sit
together at the kitchen table drinking coffee. They're laughing because
Walter made a joke about coffee and "grounds for divorce." My
mother throws back her head, shakes her hair back and forth. When he
leans his arm toward her, handle of his cup hanging from
his baby finger, she offers him a refill from the pot on the stove,
pours it all the way to the top.

In Control

In first grade Miss McCann draws the number 2 on the chalkboard between wide lines of yellow chalk. The loop rests on the bottom line. Perfect petal on a twig. "Practice drawing the number two." Cautious I draw a small square for the loop. Tiny box. Trying to form the symbol of what 1 + 1 adds up to brought a warning, as though making the loop would release a genie out of the bottle. A square kept the genie locked away. The next number in line will never move past it.

Grease Paint

My mother's gold compact has a mirror and light brown circle of
pancake make-up. She dabs powder onto her nose and cheeks with
a thin round sponge. There's a black and gold patterned circular
box of bath powder with a fluffy powder puff she's never used. In the
bathroom cabinet a small plastic case of rouge the size of a fifty-cent
piece, and lipstick in a tortoise shell case.

When I play dress ups I try on her makeup then hobble in her brown
and white spectator pumps with small holes in the tip of the toe in her
slip with lace edging. Once I covered the bathroom mirror with red
lines criss-crossing. Out of control. Face paint gone awry. Smells of
lipstick and powder became one smell; a promise broken, something
clean and formed, were it a bird, came to the window and did not stay.

Forbearance

It is summer. I'm visiting my cousins, Gay and Diane, in New Haven.
My Aunt Phyl takes us to someone's house for an outdoor party. Green
and white striped lawn chairs. Bowls of potato chips, pretzels, and
mixed nuts. People play croquet and badminton. I like it when the
mallet strikes the wooden ball and watch as it rolls through metal
wickets. The yellow, green, red, blue, or orange stripe on the ball
matches the stripe around the handle of the mallet. While my cousins
play I sit in a chair beneath the green umbrella. A breeze crosses my
face then moves on. I imagine it traveled to wherever my mother is,
touched her face, and then came back to me.

II

on tiptoe proceed over eggshells where balance eludes
morning & noon while night illumines the one-way
street glassine as water she walks on

Joan reading to Joanie and Susie
Gardner, Massachusetts
Worcester Gazette 1950

Dance Little Dolly

My sister is two. She turns in circles, shakes her arms. My father claps his hands. Her red corduroy overalls with puppies printed on them snap shut. Scuffed white leather shoes. She rocks back and forth, one foot then the other when he claps his hands, sings, "Dance little dolly with a hole in your stocking, dance by the light of the moon." She twirls around, laughs and smiles when she hears him say, "She can dance. She's a dancer; just look at her dance."

Dusk

Birds Eye. Corn and lima beans. Frosty white box she pulls out of the freezer inside the fridge. Saucepan. Spoon. The kitchen fills with light from the overhead fixture. Dark has fallen. Late December. I watch Howdy Doody in the room at the end of the hallway. She breaks into song. "Maybe I will meet him Sunday, maybe Monday, maybe not. . . . Still I'm sure to meet him one day, maybe Tuesday will be. . . .my good news day."

my   good   news   day

Each word set down like a plate on the table. Each plate the same size between the fork on the left, knife and spoon on the right.

She serves the yellow corn and pale green lima beans.

"Succotash," she says.

Her hair is light brown. I know she misses him.

Happenstance

Skinned knee. Stubbed toe. Bruises black and blue. Dog bite.
Cat scratch. An egg swells up on your head. Sprained thumb.
Trip, bump, twist. Nothing serious, yet it stings. Shock of blood.
Suck your knee. Salt when sky turned its back.

Luminescent

Cliff LaPierre goes to my father's church; he owns an appliance store downtown. One morning he delivers a new kitchen range. My mother watches him roll it in on a dolly then ease it onto the linoleum. He slides it into the space where the old stove was. It's a GE and will last for years. The white surface gleams like the one where stars make circles around each other on TV when the man at the desk on General Electric Theater talks about "the kitchen of the future."

I ask Cliff to sign my Autograph Book. He writes, "To a swell girl, from CLP." My mother stands in the doorway between the kitchen and hallway watching him work, elbow in her right hand, chin cupped in her left. I know she doesn't want Cliff to leave.

When the stove's hooked up he says, "You're all set," then touches my head. He walks toward the door and closes it behind him. The dolly makes a bumping sound down the front steps.

My mother and I stay in the kitchen with the new stove. Do not speak. We wait as they wait at Lourdes. For a sign. For the blessed light.

Becalmed

I'm in bed because I have mumps on the left side. The bulge below my left jawbone aches. I'm running a temperature and have been in bed for four days. On my lap a tray with small bowls of Easter egg dye and wire circle with a handle to hold the eggs I dip into the dye. My mother brings a bowl of nine hard-boiled eggs. When I finish she sets them on the windowsill to dry. Some have mixed colors; blue and pink, or green and yellow. Tomorrow's Easter. I won't be able to wear the navy circle skirt with a matching short-sleeved bolero my mother made for me. White cotton top, a thin navy ribbon tied under the collar. My yellow straw hat with a wide brim goes with the outfit. I had mumps on the right side last year but didn't dye Easter eggs.

Purity

My mother cuts out white flannel she sews on her black Singer sewing machine. As she holds the fabric flat the presser foot hums joining the seams. Gathered yoke and long sleeves gathered at the cuffs. When I put it on my mother says I look "like an angel."

I feel holy in my nightgown. One night in the living room my mother and I are sitting down. My sister plays with toys on the floor. I feel ethereal and wise. That morning my mother had expected me to do something. It felt harsh. She did not smile or say I was "wonderful."

I spoke about the morning, said, "That's no way to treat a child."

She looked down, sorry for what she had said. I felt encircled, as if a halo surrounded me.

Caged

I walk to the matinee downtown with Patty Morris and Mary Ann
Schneider. Usher in a red uniform, brass buttons on the jacket shows
us to our seats. She holds a flashlight even though we can still see.
Lights dim as the heavy purple curtain pulls back, "Previews of
Coming Attractions." A man and women kiss. Gangsters with guns,
cowboys chasing a stagecoach. Every movie is "Wonderful," "Best
to Ever Hit the Screen." *Caged* is in black and white. Behind bars
women have long fingernails painted a dark color. Dark lipstick.
Something terrible is going on. I hide my eyes. Patty jabs me with
her elbow, "You're missing everything." I peek between my fingers.
Iron doors clang when they lock the women up. The jail warden large
and cold has lots of keys on a circle looped through her belt.

Household

Our kitchen has a wooden table and chairs where I eat my Cheerios.
I watch them float in the bowl of milk. Clock on the wall has a red
rim. Red numbers. The red hands don't move.

Black ants scurry around the faucets and sink. Antennae wave from
shiny black heads. They trail in from the back porch, march into
the kitchen and up to the sink. My mother doesn't want to put ant
poison out.

When an ant carried a crumb almost as big as its body across the
kitchen counter my mother called to me. She said it was industrious
like the ant storing food for winter while the grasshopper sang away
the days.

At night mice search for food, leave black droppings all over the
kitchen. My mother sets wooden mousetraps, small square of cheese
for bait. Sometimes I hear the trap snap over the neck of a mouse. One
morning a mouse lay in the trap, thin pink tail, white whiskers, veins
showed through its ears. White teeth for gnawing.

Once when its foot got caught in the trap a mouse screamed in pain.
My mother let it go. She didn't want it to suffer, but we had to get
rid of them. They were taking over the house.

Sufficient

It snowed last night. Outside the air is cold. I begin to make a snow
horse, roll a large ball of snow then try to shape it. Legs begin to form,
then the neck. Its head doesn't look like a horse. It's hard. Only half
my size, it looks more like a dog. I smooth it with my wool mittens.
My face numb, the sky dark gray. My mother watches me from the
kitchen window. I pretend I don't see her. I want to do this by myself.
Alone.

Backbone

Walking an hour a day with a book on your head will improve your
posture. This is what they do at the Kathleen Peck Modeling School.
Ads show a slender young woman, hair tied back with a black ribbon.
She smiles, her shoulders and spine straight. My grandfather says
to imagine someone's pulling me up by the hair. This is the way to
have good posture. Aunt Phyllis says I slump and will become round-
shouldered. I imagine myself, shoulders like melons, face flat against
the table. "You look like a question mark," another aunt says. My
father raises his curved finger slowly when he sits at the end of the
dining room table. His nostrils flare. After my sister's ballet recital her
teacher, Margaret Sundsten, walks to the microphone to thank us for
coming. Perfect posture, her neck like a swan.

Finery

We sew doll clothes. Gingham fabric, sheer batiste, polished cotton,
crinkled seersucker, white eyelet, yellow pique. My Madame
Alexander doll has brown hair. My mother makes a white eyelet
dress trimmed in red bias tape and red ric-rac. The back fastens with
two snaps, pocket on the gathered skirt in the shape of a heart. I push
her in my baby carriage. It was beside the tree on Christmas morning,
just like a real baby carriage except smaller, with white wheels and
a gray hood that folds up and down. I push it around the house and
down the sidewalk, keep my doll's clothes safe inside a red toy trunk
with a silver lock and key.

Visitor

My Aunt Jean graduated *cum laude* from Mount Holyoke. Later they
asked her to be president, but she said, "No." She worked in the
library of the Lawrenceville School where Uncle Tom taught English.
Summers they lived in Jaffrey up the road from my grandparent's
farmhouse in the house Tom built with timbers from an old ship.

Tom rowed on Harvard crew; his Harvard chair is next to the stairs.
He was in the Navy in World War II, and their red house felt snug like
a ship. In the *Colorado* Room a stone fireplace. All over the house
clipper ships Tom constructed inside bottles. Jean hooked rugs for the
bathroom with whales against light blue backgrounds. They call the
kitchen "the galley," tiny hallway, everything in place.

She makes stewed pears and chicken with peas. For breakfast Jean
cooks poached eggs; drops them into boiling water until they form
frilly edges with a film over the yolk. She serves them with a stack
of toast cut in half and glasses of fresh squeezed orange juice. After
breakfast she clears the table, scrapes the dishes, washes and dries
them, then puts them away.

Tom reads aloud from books stacked on the table. Poetry and
Shakespeare. He has a deep voice. While she listens Jean does her
sewing. Every year she organizes the Jaffrey Fair. When we move
across the country at Christmas she sends potholders, pine scented
sachets, and stitched pillows "from the Fair."

Sometimes Jean makes thin crisp sugar cookies with grated lemon
peel. They turn out this way because she uses real butter not
margarine. She keeps them in a red and white tin with a red top
after she folds wax paper over the cookies, "tight," she says, "to
keep the air out."

Maestro

Mary Hartline conducts the *Super Circus* band in her short dress
with a white song note on the front. She wears white boots with
tassels, and has long blonde hair. She holds a thin white baton
and faces away from the band while she moves it up and down or
to the side. She smiles as she brings music into the television even
though people playing the instruments can't see her hands or follow
the baton.

Vanquished

Caterpillars in gathered pockets of my plaid dress crawl onto my skirt. Five appear on my dress the day Joey Anderson asks how can I stand to have them all over me?

I collect them. They're my pets. I take them home to a jar with holes punched into the lid. Twigs for resting, green leaves to eat. Two caterpillars have spun cocoons onto the twig. The others almost cover the bottom of the jar on the dresser next to my bed.

One night I dream they've escaped. Caterpillars over my pillow, under my sheets. I scream, "Get rid of the caterpillars."

"Are you sure this is what you want me to do?" my mother asks. "What will you think in the morning?" I cry for her to take them out of the house.

In the morning empty jar on the dresser. Twigs gone and the leaves.

Plight

I was three when we lived in the Seminary and she wanted to throw me out the window. I was a new baby in Franklin, Pennsylvania and my father was in the war. She wanted to throw me into the burning fireplace. She laughs when she says this. I hear these stories for years starting when I'm six.

Contained

On TV in a show about a woman and little girl, they both live in Iron
Lungs. They breathe for them. In and out. Up and down. They see
what's going on in a mirror above their heads. The man who explains
about the Iron Lungs says they're paralyzed because of polio. This
means they can't walk or breathe on their own. The Iron Lung is their
body now. The woman and little girl smile and talk about being able
to live at home. The Lung sounds like a huge animal. The little girl
has a ribbon in her hair and little white bear hanging from the top of
her mirror. I wonder about their legs and arms, feet and hands. Is the
rest of them warm. Is it lonely inside the Lung. My mother says it's
wonderful they can have this machine to breathe for them. The way
she says it makes me want to just lie down, like the girl.

Sunday Dinner

After church we have dinner at the Colonial Hotel. A man who's a
deacon in my father's church owns it and never gives him a bill. My
mother always orders prawns. I have a shrimp cocktail in a tall glass
dish, and deep-fried clam strips. My sister's in a high chair and eats
some of my mother's dinner. Before we sit down I see cloth napkins
folded beneath our knife and spoon, flowers in the middle of the table.
My mother and father study the menu. There's music playing, and
I ask, "Why can't it always be like this?" But they don't say anything
because they're waiting for the waiter to come to our table in his white
jacket and black bow tie to ask, "What can I bring you?"

Close Call

My mother almost drowned when she was a girl. In summer she swam out too far. Her leg cramped up. She froze with fear. Sank twice. Just before she went down for the third and final time a man saw terror on her face. He dove in then pulled her in to shore. She would have drowned beneath the darkness.

Departure

Before driving to Rhode Island to visit my grandparents we wait;
my sister and I in the back seat, our father behind the steering wheel.
Inside the house our mother checks the stove then patrols each room
making sure our father's cigarette butts are out. Sometimes she pours
water into the ashtrays. He honks the horn. Between his teeth we hear,
"What's she *doing* in there?"

Finally she opens the front door, double checks to make sure it's
locked. When she gets in the car she turns around to smile at us then
asks if our doors are locked. Silence all the way to Providence.

III

when it falls over water this time I will see you

Joanie and Susie ages 10 and 4
Christmas card photo
Gardner, Massachusetts 1953

Mirrored

The staircase to the right of the first floor entry hall turns left onto
the second floor landing. I slide down the banister's polished wood
backwards holding on. The top floor's white rails keep us from falling.
These stairs have the feeling of ascent, of rising. I trip down them as
fast as I can. A mirror hangs in front of where they begin.

I saw myself in the mirror once, my hair secured in pony tails with
rubber bands. This face surprised me, a child rounding the bed on her
way to some destination. The fleeting image lasted because the mirror
was there.

Motto

My Brownie uniform's made from thin brown cotton with short sleeves, buttons down the front. Woven brown belt. Two pockets on the bodice. My hat's a brown beanie, felt, with a tiny brownie stamped on the front. On Wednesdays I wear my uniform to school.

Goodnow Pearson's Department Store has a window display, supplies for Girl Scouts and Boy Scouts. The *Girl Scout Manual* with the motto: "Be Prepared," jackknife blades folded into a green handle, corkscrew, can opener. Mess Kit, pan, bowl, plate, cup, and silverware stacked inside a green bag.

Wednesdays we meet in the church basement. Mrs. Needham holds up two fingers in a V; be quiet and pay attention.

I sit very still in my Brownie uniform. Brown shoes, light brown socks, on their brown fold-over cuffs the image of a Brownie, I wait for the meeting to begin. I belong where supplies are stacked then put away, with a compass and silver whistle to keep from getting lost.

Grace

"Who's going to recite the blessing?" My father sits at the head of the table in a chair with wooden arms. He looks at my mother, my sister, and me.

Our fingers lace between our hands folded in front of our plates. We bow our heads, wait for someone else to say:

> *Father we thank thee for this food,*
> *Help us to be kind of good. Amen*

It's like church, but we're in our house where my mother prepared dinner on a night when my father sits at the dining room table. We pretend it's this way every night when we say the blessing. Eyes closed, we say "Amen" together.

I want to ask my father why he keeps waking us up at night if he believes what the blessing says.

If my sister or I don't say it our mother recites:

> *Blessed art Thou Oh Lord*
> *Who bringest forth bread from the ground.*

It's a relief when she does.

Cure

When I have a scratchy throat I stay home from school. While I lie in bed my mother brings bowls of ice cream; vanilla or Neapolitan. I let it melt then drink it from the bowl. In fifth grade I miss fifty-four days of school. The doctor says I need to have my tonsils taken out.

On the operating table the nurse who teaches Sunday school in my father's church puts a cone over my nose. It's ether. She tells me, "Count to ten." A strange smell makes everything wobble and loop. I fall into a hole where she asks, "How do you like our perfume?" When I wake up my throat's on fire. The nurse says, "You can have all the ice cream you want." I can't swallow and don't want ice cream.

Reckless

On Saturday Carole Rahaim and I ride our bikes to the Woodland Spa.
Outside there's a phone booth and pay phone. I call my mother, tell
her I'm kidnapped.

Two men with a gun forced me into their car and tied me up, but
I found a way to undo the knots and snuck out when they went into
the store.

I hear terror in her voice. She starts to cry. Thin ribbons flutter.

Carole giggles, covers her mouth with her hand. My mother says,
"I hear Carole. Are you pretending?"

I say, "Yes," I tell her there are no men. We're at The Spa to buy
Fudgsicles.

She'll be angry when I get home. Fudgsicles cost a nickel. I buy three.
Eat them all.

Magnum Opus

The cover of the paint-by-number kit says, "Every man a Rembrandt."
Inside ten tubes of oil paints, two brushes, and printed white canvas
with a ballerina on point, arms arced over her shoulders. She looks
like a jig-saw puzzle; every section with a number lets you know what
tube of oil paint will fill it in.

I lay newspapers on the dining room table, squeeze blobs of paint onto
tin can lids. First the green toe-shoes, then her legs. When I move back
from the canvas the ballerina's leg muscles stand out, oblong shapes
light tan and cream. It takes a long time to fill the spaces. Sometimes
paint won't stay inside the lines. I finish filling in the light and dark
green tutu, then stop.

My mother says I stopped at just the right time.

Later she hangs my painting on the wall. She says someday we'll
frame it.

Halloween

I'm a ghost for the third year in a row. My mother cut two holes for eyes out of the white sheet I wear over my head. Slits for my arms.

She hemmed it below my knees so I won't trip. I carry a white pillowcase to hold my candy. Carole and I go up and down both sides of Woodland Avenue, Green Street, and Chestnut Street. We knock on doors. "Trick or treat." Leaves from the sidewalk cover our shoes.

Mrs. Farnsworth offers us paper cups filled with apple juice, sticky popcorn balls wrapped in red cellophane tied with a string.

Instrument

Our wooden music box plays "The Blue Bells of Scotland" and "Loch Lomond." On top there's a painting of soft purple green hills and meadows, a feeling of water and light. It says "hand painted" on the bottom next to the key.

When I lift the lid I see the insides under a pane of glass. I wind the key and songs begin to play. The small metal cylinder turns while little metal strips reach out and catch on its tiny hinges.

My mother says Scotland is a country attached to England, but with more fog and roads that never stop.

Inspiration

On the way to School Street School I walk by the beauty shop on the first floor of the Woodland Spa. Taped to the window posters with perfectly coiffed hair-dos, waves and curls that don't look real. Strapless evening gowns, cheeks aglow. Pale rouge like movie stars in dusky light.

Something about them informs my reading of Cherry Ames Student Nurse books I borrow from the library: "Eighteen-year-old Cherry Ames takes the first steps on the road to a nursing career as she begins three years of training at Spencer Hospital," and *A Date for Marcy* by Rosemary du Jardin. Identical twins pretend to be each other fooling the boy who believes he's dating one when he's really dating her sister. On the dust jacket two teenage girls with perfect features wear bright red lipstick.

The perfection of hair and features is what I desire when I ask for a Nurse's Kit for my ninth birthday. Cardboard case with handle and clasp, compartments hold plastic thermometer, stethoscope, crisp white paper cap, a bottle of multi-colored candy pills.

Holding the Nurse's Kit I feel capable. Competent, beautiful and confident like Cherry Ames in her white apron, and striped uniform as she holds her clipboard and sharp pencil. Even though I consume the bottle of candy pills right after receiving my Nurse's Kit, I carry it for days, offering to take my mother or sister's temperature or check their pulse to make us well.

Crepes

My mother cooks French pancakes in the black iron skillet. Melts
butter, then pours in batter stirred from eggs, milk, flour, sugar,
and salt. She sprinkles the thin pancakes with confectionery sugar.
Sometimes she rolls them up before she adds the sugar.

It takes us all morning to finish the batch. My sister likes pancakes
the size of silver dollars, and counts how many she eats. I ask for
ones that cover the bottom of the pan.

Ballast

After school I turn on the black and white TV to watch *The Gabby Hayes Show* on NBC. He's a cowboy, gray beard and hat folded straight up in front. He wears a vest, plaid shirt, and bandana around his neck. When he holds up a Mounds Bar and says, "Go right down to the store and buy yourself one; there's nothin' like that chocolate covered coconut for an after school treat," I want to run to the Woodland Spa to unwrap it like he did. Big bite of coconut mixing with the chocolate.

He says, "You can divide a Three Musketeers Bar three ways with your two best friends." The bar's a rectangle, soft light brown candy covered in chocolate with two lines that dip to break into three separate pieces. Sometimes I have a Three Musketeers Bar ready when Gabby unwraps his, break it into three sections and eat them all.

My sister's in the kitchen with my mother. I'm far away listening to Gabby Hayes say, "Hi there all you young whipper snappers," as I wait to watch movies of cowboys shooting up the town before they ride to the hideout. Then Gabby unwraps an Almond Joy divided in two parts on black paper trays.

Hearts

My Ballroom Dancing class Valentine's Day party will have a prize for the best costume. My mother's sewing mine from a white sheet. The short skirt's like Mary Hartline's on *Super Circus*. The sleeveless top attaches to the skirt. When she fits the top and skirt she says, "Stand very still." With pins in her mouth it's hard to talk. She tugs on the skirt to make sure the hem hangs straight. Her black sewing machine sits on its cabinet, light left on while she turns up the hem.

She cuts two huge hearts out of stiff red paper, loops red yarn through small holes punctured through the tops. She pastes white lace around them, attaches a small bouquet of felt violets to the lower side of the heart covering my front. The valentine hearts reach from my neck to below my waist.

She sews a white cap, attaches a red paper heart to the back.

I win the prize for best costume. Runners up are Kenneth Bonk, Robin Hood with a bow and arrow, and Brian Sims, white-faced clown with a mop of orange hair.

I'm wearing red lipstick to match the heart. In *The Gardner News* photograph my hearts and lipstick look dark.

Wonder Bread

Soft in white plastic. Red, blue, yellow balloons. White bread. Brown crust. Fresh but not like food. Fresh as a lie you swallow.

On the Summer Air

The Stephen Foster Songbook's yellow cloth cover is open on the piano. My mother plays, sings, "Beautiful Dreamer, and "I Dream of Jeanie with the Light Brown Hair."

Sad and slow, she doesn't smile. Everyone in the songs is asleep. Women with long hair float around like ghosts.

Sometimes I look through it by myself, study the words and illustrations; "Old Black Joe" and "Massa's in De Cold Cold Ground." Men in the pictures stoop.

My father's church in Oxford is white with a steeple. Our parsonage is white, three wooden columns in front like the ones in"Old Black Joe" But our house isn't huge like the one in the picture.

My mother says Stephen Foster lived in the deep South where he wrote songs about plantations and slaves. I wonder who are the old men bent over with dark skin, and why do they look so tired?

Family Visit

At Girl Scout camp I belong to Merry Maids, the group for ten-year-old girls. It's Sunday afternoon. My mother, father, and sister drove to Camp Collier to visit me. We sit on a blanket over pine needles surrounded by pine trees. Earlier I performed a swimming routine. Six of us swam backwards kicking our feet and reading newspapers.

My father's lying on his back, eyes closed, one arm over his chest. My mother sits with knees drawn up, arms around her legs. Her head lies sideways on her knees. My sister is four and leans against the tree. I smell the pine needles. During Rest Time in the afternoon I write home about braiding a lariat to hold a whistle. Thin strips of shiny red and white plastic I'm weaving to wear around my neck.

After dark we sit around a campfire roasting marshmallows to add to S'Mores made from Hershey Bars and graham crackers. We sing songs, "One nine-five-four at Collier Camp, no other year the same." My favorite is "The Ash Grove" when our voices break into harmony, "Tis there where the black bird is cheerfully singing." Path at twilight toward a dark grove of trees. This is what I'm thinking as I sit with my family close to the circle of canvas tents.

Coloring Books

Movie star. Gown and furs. Snow White. Cinderella. Bo-Peep holds her crook. Page after page outfits and costumes outlined in black. Only lips are colored in, as though the red mouths could sing, could tell the truth, and if not that, be noticed, not ignored like the rest of the story.

Naming

My mother's crying, my father's voice a slow cruel train. At night
I count ten girls' names for every letter of the alphabet until I fall
asleep.

Amy, Abigail, Ann, Annette, Alice, Alexa. . .

Amanda Krebs sits in the desk in front of mine, skirt with shamrocks
her favorite.She's good in math, has a pencil box with sharpened
pencils and two erasers. I watch Mr. Mattick write on the board under
the section where he wrote "Assignments" the first day of school.

He erases the rest but never "Assignments." His eraser's nicked some
letters, but we know what it means: due dates, homework. It's our
responsibility to copy page numbers and complete these problems for
the next day. Amanda finishes the math book. Someone already taught
her. I never understand math even when I pretend I do.

Candy, Cathy, Cynthia, Christine, Celeste. . .

Cecily in nursery school in the Seminary. White ringlets, braces on her
legs. Her father carried her on his shoulders, said she was "light as a
feather." She laughed and held on to his hair.

I wished I had leg braces, but nothing was wrong with me.

Clarkie's Pond

Green Street runs behind our backyard. Clarkie lives on it in a small
red house, his pond beside it. In winter he hoses it down, makes it
smooth so whoever wants to can ice skate there.

He keeps a fire going to warm us. Sometimes laces on my white
leather ice skates freeze. Usually I get one lace untied and totter home.

I'm supposed to be home before dark. When I walk down Green Street
toward our house I see light in the kitchen window. Our house is built
into a hill. Stairs made from flat stones lead up to back of the house,
then wooden stairs to the kitchen door.

Before I climb the stone stairs I stand next to the garage, look up.
My breath white clouds. Mittens crack when I make a fist.

Tradition

We string popcorn chains with cranberries onto thread. This means we use needles that could drop on the rug, get lost until we step on them and they enter our blood stream. Go straight to our heart. But tonight we sit on the couch in the living room. My mother puts the thread in her mouth, stiffens it with her saliva. She rubs it between her thumb and forefinger so she can slip it through the eye of the needle.

As we work we eat some of the popcorn in a large bowl on the table. My father popped it in a Paul Revere saucepan with a copper bottom. He heated the oil until three or four kernels began to pop, then poured in the rest. Some never pop. Black kernels on the bottom. He didn't add butter or salt because of the chains.

It's hard to get the needle through the popcorn. Sometimes it breaks. I string four or five cranberries for every kernel of popcorn. My mother doesn't notice. My sister sucks her thumb.

It takes a long time. I want to stop, but this is getting ready for Christmas. Our tree's in the corner, box of glass ornaments beside it. We'll hang tinsel from the branches after we hang the popcorn chains. Ornaments go on after the lights. The colored lights are tangled. My father has a hard time straightening the wires.

My mother hums "Silent Night" and "O Little Town of Bethlehem." Our fingers are red from the berries. Christmas feels far away even though we have our tree.

Vacancy

It's 1952. My father's been "called up" to serve in the army for a year.
Jeanne Leland will rent an upstairs room while he's away.

She's a teacher; her room's clean and neat. A green pixie made of
porcelain sits cross-legged on the table next to her bed.

Jeanne buys groceries for my mother. Most of the time she stays in
her room to work at her desk. Sometimes I look at the light under
her door.

At Christmas my father mails a box from Germany. He sends me a
bride doll and music box I wind with a key. Gray wooden box covered
with glass. Three kittens dance on a rooftop; cat perched on the chimney
plays the fiddle, wears a scarf and stovepipe hat. When I wind the
music box the kittens' arms and legs move up and down. The fiddler's
bow goes back and forth. Windows below have filled with yellow
light, night behind and above the kittens. A few stars, bright moon.

One day I dare a boy to push me off the high stone wall. Dare him
again. He shoves me off the railing. I land hard. Hit my head.

Two girls help me home. Everything whirling.

When I get to the door my mother looks worried, tells me to lie down.
She calls the doctor, "Don't fall asleep."

The doctor says I need to rest, but to stay awake. "If you fall asleep
you might never wake up."

I want to not wake up over the roof where the fiddler plays.

IV

sky's a gray haunt. No one answers.
In the story once there was a village, house
with an open door

Joan by the hearth in the parsonage,
Gardner, Massachusetts 1953

Incendiary

Flannel is flammable. So is batiste. Sun through a window, nightgowns catch on fire. Spark. Electric cord or outlet. Lace of fear in summer heat. Shimmer in the light of noon.

Banana on the refrigerator turns black. Shrivels to leathery rot. I watch it day after day. Don't take it down or put it in the garbage.

The banana will not catch fire. It epitomizes stasis. Except for the withering. It is a sigh. Expulsion. A flattening. Tires on a truck in the cornfield. When nothing moves there is no tension. No comings or goings and it's good to see you because you left.

Mid-afternoon. Away from the stove I wear a gingham yellow checked skirt gathered with a wide stiff waistband. If I catch fire I'll burn yellow, orange, red, and gold. Later, thin blue flame. Blue where it's hottest. Where I stop.

Attire

Sunday she wears red tights to church with her green print blouse and black skirt. Women of the congregation disapprove; she doesn't dress like a minister's wife. Red tights sag at the ankles like a clown.

Daily News

The paper comes and my mother reads of a bus crash in India. Twenty people died. Missed the turn. Sailed over the rail. She clutches the paper. Holds it over her heart. She cries out as if she knew the passengers, as if she'd been the one hurtling over the embankment.

Fallout

Gym class. Locker room. Wooden benches, showers, gray tile floor. After we change our clothes Miss Thrailkill takes attendance. Then we go to the gym to pick teams for volleyball. Miss Thrailkill wrote "D" for Demerit after my name. My wrinkled gym shorts and blouse. Our PE "uniform" represents our school.

When I asked my mother where they were she pointed to the wicker laundry basket; heap of damp towels, socks, my father's shirts. "I'll get them all lined up today."

Flagging

Drifts then sweeps, snow falls or swells to white sky. I trudge, pull each foot up then out. Set it down. Start again. The tired wants to stay but where. There were supposed to be red boots for walking, red mittens with snowflakes, a hat's two pom-poms dangling from crocheted strings. Snow keeps falling. The walking slow. This is winter. I am not brave. Cold is close. I hold my ears. No one knows this. No one.

Math Test

When she sits down to eat with my sister and me she asks about my day. Mine was the lowest math test. I was the last one standing when Miss Hayes read our names and scores outloud.

"You must have gotten that from me. I wasn't any good at math either." She smiles at me when she says this.

Heartsick

In seventh grade I talk to Dennis Foster every morning at the bus stop. One morning he says, "Give up."

Dennis is thin. He wears tight jeans and lives in Apple Valley. He combs his blond hair in stiff waves with VO-5. The waves separate into spaces between the teeth in his comb.

I hoped he'd be my boyfriend. Watched for him in the halls.

The day Dennis tells me I run home in tears wearing a plaid cotton skirt and matching top with puff sleeves. My white Joyce Stepladders for spring are scuffed. I fall onto the couch crying too hard to talk.

My mother comes out of the kitchen to comfort me. Years later she can still see me through the window in black-watch plaid. My cotton skirt filled with the wind as I ran.

Chanticleer

My mother's rooster in watercolors is taped to the wall behind the
toilet in the bathroom/laundry room next to the rec-room where
I watch television. Deep red wattles, blue-green feathers, yellow
clawed feet. Purple eye, orange dot at the center. Upstairs a
woodblock, abstract church steeple where it shouldn't be, angles
and shadows lurking. My father doodles millions of lines and dots,
quickly sketches cartoon men; bowties, glasses. Stiff shocks of hair.
I draw profiles of girls with smooth page-boy hairdos and Mickey
Mouse by writing CS that turns into his nose and mouth. Whenever
I draw my mother says I'm an artist. Even the snowman in sixth
grade before we moved to Bellevue. Miss Gilhooley mimeographed
them in purple lines. Every one looked the same.

La Mer

The summer I'm twelve we're on vacation in Seaside, Oregon. My mother wears my white one-piece bathing suit with gray kittens and red trim. Its blousy bottom resembles short bloomers. Red straps of the halter-top knot behind her neck. She carries a rolled up pink towel under her arm. I wear my green Girl Scout shorts with a white stripe down each side and green and white striped T-shirt.

She looks toward the ocean. Too big, too much to hold. Yet we are here; my mother, father, sister and I, walking down the beach at sunset.

Wet sand reflects the setting sun. In black, yellow, and white plaid swimming trunks my father stands up to his knees in the surf. My mother appears alarmed. We cannot venture into the waves where everyone splashes and runs. I smell smoke from beach fires where people toast marshmallows on long pointed sticks and know it's time to go back to The Waves motel. Under its name in blue neon white waves skip back and forth like blinking eyes.

Ocean waves roll in, hit the sand, then pull out like someone taking a breath. When I ask, " Our family is lucky aren't we mom?" she smiles, says, "Yes." Holds my hand the way she always does, squeezing my fingers for luck.

Menarche

My mother talked about her mother's first period. She thought she
was bleeding to death. Her mother never prepared her. She felt terror
when the red blood appeared. And my mother talked of the day a
black snake slithered across my grandmother's lap while she sat in
a meadow. Paralyzed with fear she watched the snake make its way
across her lap. She repeated these stories as if for the first time. My
grandmother as a child. A summer morning. Light and shadows
filtered onto the white porch. Warmth of the blood, strange intrusion
like the snake. Something gone wrong. Her body mute. Unable to say,
This is a beginning. Threshold. A day to remember.

Sparkling Clean

When the Fuller Brush man rings the doorbell my mother invites
him in. He opens his leather bag to take out brushes he lines up on
the table. Some to clean your nails, others; small, medium, and large,
to brush your hair. Brushes to remove lint from black dresses, scrub
brushes to clean the floor. He explains how bristles are strong yet
flexible enough to reach into corners to remove dirt or food collected
there.

My mother listens. She tells him how wonderful the brushes are,
then offers him some coffee. After he puts them back in his bag he sits
down at the table, takes out an order form. My mother will take
a hairbrush with natural bristles, and a white nailbrush; black bristles
and handle to hold while you scrub your hands or clean your nails.
Bristles for nails along one side of the brush are in three separate rows.
On the other side, bristles cover the brush. Jasper, our Golden Lab,
will chew the handle until it looks like a strong machine crushed it.

After he completes the order form and gives my mother a copy, the
Fuller Brush man tells her he's studying to be a teacher. My mother
says she'll order three more brushes, then asks for the catalog he
was going to leave on the table. She turns its shiny pages with
photographs. "Tell me about them again," she says, "suggest the
ones you think I need."

Keeping Score

Walking home from Junior High I pass Bellevue Square and stop
at Frederick & Nelson's. I usually buy something with the F & N
charge card in my father's name; scrapbook, charm bracelet, cologne,
a new outfit.

At the end of the month he receives a fat envelope of yellow receipts
and invoice for my purchases: dresses; sleeveless, red and white
peppermint striped; powder blue, dropped waistline edged in white
trim.

When I show her the striped dress my mother says, "It's better he
spends money on this than on vodka." I feel noble and brave.

Fetch

Our tri-level house is in "The Circle," a round street of Bell and Valdez tri-levels, split-levels, some houses just on the ground. Jasper brings the neighbors' doormats home, drops them in our yard or by our front door. He's a retriever. It's his instinct to fetch birds for hunters. My mother says he thinks doormats are something he's supposed to discover and bring home to us. Jasper is a working dog.

Once he brought home a large Oriental rug rolled up and tied with rope at both ends. He stood next to it wagging his tail. My mother kept patting his head saying, "I just don't see how you ever got such a big rug home."

It's my job to return them. I knock on the door then ask if whoever lives there is missing their doormat. Some of the neighbors say we should fence our dog in even though I always bring their doormats back.

Our doormat's made from black rubber with "Welcome" in white letters. Jasper took it to the back yard, chewed the corner until it said "elcome."

We still use it, even after we move to Bainbridge Island. When the doorbell rings my sister and I say "Elcome, elcome ome," just before we open the door.

Tutelage

My mother taught me how to put on nylons. First, wear gloves so you won't snag them. Then roll one nylon all the way down to your toe and place your toes into the point of the foot. Slowly unroll the nylon up your foot past your ankle, and all the way up your leg. Then do the other leg. Take care putting on nylons because they run easily. They're delicate and expensive. I need to do as much as I can to make them last and last.

My mother taught me to scramble eggs. First crack the eggs on the edge of a bowl, then break them into it. Beat them together with a fork and a little milk, then add a pinch of salt. Heat the black iron skillet until it's hot and pour the eggs in. Cook them quickly with a spatula, move them around folding them over. Don't let them sit in the skillet.

Then she lifts them out onto the oval serving plate with red and blue flowers. Light and yellow, they taste good.

Entrée

We're having Poor Man's Pie. My mother carries it to the table with her green and orange oven mitts.

It's made from ground beef she browns with onions then puts in a casserole dish. She fixes mashed potatoes to cover the ground beef. This is "the crust." When it comes out of the oven the potatoes are crisp on top. She puts ketchup in the middle before she cooks the pie.

There are sixteen bottles of ketchup in the refrigerator. They stand next to each other, some with an inch of ketchup or less. Others half or a third full, some just opened. All Heinz 57. She puts one on the table if we want more ketchup with our Poor Man's Pie.

When I say I'll clean up the kitchen she says, "That's wonderful sweetheart," as if she's throwing someone a bridal bouquet and it's a summer afternoon. As I gather up dishes to stack next to the sink she watches from the kitchen table where she's drinking a cup of instant coffee and twisting her foot. Sometimes she weaves her fingers together.

I wonder if I'll ever finish washing the silverware. The knives, forks, and spoons don't match. Some have the letter "B" for our last name engraved on the handle. They used to belong to my grandmother. Others have small stars ordered with box tops from laundry detergent.

When I wash all the dishes, silverware, and pans I dry then put them away, wipe the pink Formica, and sweep the floor. There are two pewter glasses on the windowsill with sour milk. I don't take them down or wash them. My mother holds her coffee cup to her chin, says the kitchen has never looked so beautiful. I have a touch for domesticity and am an artist. I hear her as I take off the apron then hang it on the hook just above the basement stairs.

S.O.S.

There's no way out of this language. Tongue curls in a knot, keeps on talking. Wake up. Begin the day. Except the stairs are broken. Streets have filled with whizzing cars. Turn off the stove; check then check and check it again.

She patrols the house. Staying alive. Dented cans mean botulism, muscles turned to stone. Rusty nail. Tetanus enters the scratch on your leg. Rabies in saliva, the neighbor's dog. You foam at the mouth until it's too late. Undercooked pork means trichinosis. It takes six weeks to die.

Sugar Lumps

I suck on sugar cubes. Blue, white, and gold pitcher in the basin on
my grandmother's dresser. Silver mirror, white bristled hair brush,
pin cushion's bejeweled hat pins. Sweetness dissolves on my tongue. I
swallow as if somehow kindness were part of this atmosphere, my
grandmother's smile so much like my father's. This magic tempts
me to believe she loves me, strong capable woman rinsing a chicken
under the faucet. I watch her iron white shirts until the starched
creased sleeves hang down stiff as white knives. I am in the house
where I visit my grandmother wanting her to love me, knowing she's
angry behind the smile. I answer with one of my own. She knows I
took the sugar as snow falls onto the sill where I stare into the empty
bird feeder's glass, fire in winter sun.

Hygiene

After I wash and dry my hair my mother worries if I go outside. A damp head could lead to strep throat, Scarlet Fever, and heart murmur.

When Babs Nichols tells her about Minipoo dry shampoo my mother announces it will save water and keep us from going outdoors with wet heads. The blue cylinder of Minipoo has a pale aqua background, the head of a woman wearing a clip-on earring. Red hair drifts around to the back and matches her lipstick.

My mother reads to my sister and me about "the new dry way" and how this "delicately scented powder cleanses hair easily." It's "a beauty must." Removes oil and odors quickly leaving our hair "soft and lustrous." It won't "disturb our waves."

Minipoo comes with a soft white mitten my mother uses to rub in the powder. I imagine small spiders trapping the oil and odors underneath the mitten. Afterwards it's hard to get the powder out of my hair. It's stuck together, filmy when I feel it with my fingers.

"Can't shampoo? Minipoo" is probably for people who are busy or away on trips. On the back of the container it also says, "Ideal for sick room use," but that's different.

*

She spreads a thin layer of toothpaste across her toothbrush, then stands, hand on hip, left elbow pointed outward. In the other hand she clutches her toothbrush, slowly turns the bristles over her teeth, a dry scouring sound that takes a long time. When finished, she takes a drink of water, rinses out her mouth. Each cheek puffs out like a fish until she spits it into the sink washes it down the drain with a quick spurt from the tap.

She uses Stimudents to exercise her gums, orange splinter-like toothpicks packed tight into what resembles a book of matches with a green cover. She works a Stimudent back and forth between her teeth to stimulate the blood so her gums remain pink and healthy. Stimudents have a minty taste. Dr. Dean recommended them and gave her free samples.

My mother takes "a quick bath" always in the afternoon. She uses two inches of lukewarm water. A white bar of Ivory Soap floats around her.

Dark Sister

Sandra Dobson doesn't like me. Cynthia Blanchard told me in the
lunchroom. After school I tell my mother. She says this is Sandra's
dark angel talking. She needs to see it, honor it. Let it out into the
light.

We drink instant coffee in pottery cups, hand painted pinecones on
the side. She stirs her coffee until the powder dissolves. Foamy
bubbles form a circle. I do the same. She rocks back and forth in
the wooden rocking chair, cup and saucer in her lap. I think about
Sandra's dark angel, wonder if it's blind.

Confidant

When he sings "You're Nobody Till Somebody Loves You" on the radio my mother says Dean Martin's voice "opens wounds" in her heart." Hands over her breastbone she imagines riding in a gondola in Venice, my father holding her hand.

She doesn't understand why he leaves when she sits beside him on the couch. After I come home from school she tells me this while we drink our instant coffee

V

whistle through the trees

Joan Stone Age 22
Franklin, Pennsylvania 1939

Written on the back of two portraits
of Joan Stone in her early twenties:

*This lovely lady looks for things that do not exist and in her search to
find them will break faith and if you give her your heart she will return
it broken, brittle and like chunks of glass.*

Signature unreadable --

Let me stay I will make you happy.

*

*The lady has a very thin belief in God.
She is beautiful as a thousand flowers. But she really does not put
a premium on a realistic love.*

*Yet there have been times when she was gentle, unselfish, and
loveable. I have always loved her even when she hurt me.*

Signature unreadable

*gathers, hems, tucks, batiste, smocking, scissors, cross-stitch, empire
waistline, yoke, bodice, dolman sleeves, scoop neck, needle, set in
sleeves, pleats, kick pleat, zipper, waistband, puffed sleeves, darts,
blind stitch, cuffs, ruffles, cording, seams, pinking shears, thread,
pattern, button, interfacing, bobbins, spools, scoop neck, raglan
sleeves, piping, ric-rac, dropped waist, thimble, collar, basting stitch,
hooks & eyes, lapels, bound buttonholes, pins, stay stitching, chintz,
pique, eyelet, floral*

Fresh Linens

The "linen closet" on the left side of the hallway leading to my mother
and father's bedroom has sliding wooden doors and is filled with stuff.
Tea-towels I gave my mother on her birthday somewhere on a back
shelf.

White pique. Embroidered violets. Tiny green leaves.

When she opens the package her eyes grow bright. "Aren't they
sweet," she says, folding each one over the curve of her wrist.
"In Paris flower vendors sell bouquets of violets wrapped in paper," as
she looks out the window above the meadow behind our house.

Reliable

Mothers on our street call me to babysit. I don't charge extra for cleaning up the kitchen, fluffing pillows, sweeping the floor, polishing the sink and faucets until they shine. I put toys away, fold laundry if it's piled in a basket beside the washer and dryer. I sing every lullaby I know to their children until they fall asleep, alphabetize books on the shelves, gather up coffee cups left around the house, soak then scrub out stains.

Then I walk to my house where my mother waits up. She asks, "Did you run cold water over your wrists? It speeds up your circulation so you won't fall asleep. In case of a fire you're the one taking care of the children you know."

Cuisine

My mother says if I don't eat my vegetables I'll die from malnutrition. She orders wheat germ through the mail from Adele Davis who knows how we should eat. She adds the brown powder to everything, says it tastes nutty and will keep us from getting cancer.

She puts a tablespoon of wheat germ in my orange juice. It doesn't dissolve, tastes chalky then sinks to a goopy ooze that sticks to the bottom of the glass even when it's washed.

After Adele Davis she orders dried seaweed from someone who knocks on the door and says it has all we need to stay healthy, to put it in meatloaf and add it to salads.

"Just mix it in," the woman says to my mother. I imagine her stirring a bowl of batter like the mother on the TV show who wears an apron over her short sleeved dress. She stirs cookie dough while her sons ask questions about problems they are having like how to buy something they can't afford and then they have to mow the lawn or take out the garbage and they forget and their father talks to them about it. The food their mother prepares will be cooked in the kitchen and served on the table in the room next to it. She keeps a bowl of fruit on it or sometimes a flower arrangement.

The pouches of dried seaweed arrive in a blue box. We eat some of it on saltines spread with Kraft Cheez Whiz.

Etsuko

My sister's pen-pal lives in Japan. She writes letters and sent
a Japanese doll in a red and gold brocade gown with a black
cummerbund. White face, eyes, mouth, and nose painted with tiny
brush strokes. Lips bright red, her black hair in tight rolls shines.
Two ivory sticks criss-cross the roll above her neck. Her glass box
has brass trim. Etsuko writes on pink stationery with scallops around
the point of the envelope.

My sister writes to Etsuko about Ashwood Elementary and where we
live. My mother talks about cherry trees in Japan and Zen monks. She
does zazen sitting and practices Woo Wei, "Doing nothing is the
highest art." She writes haiku about the crocus that suffers winter
pain before it breaks through the cold dark ground.

Etsuko sends my sister a fan. My mother unfolds it. Holds it beneath
her eyes, moves it back and forth. She says, "This is what Geisha's
do," as if she knows how it is to be a Geisha, has lived a Geisha's life
and seen cherry trees in spring even though the poem she quotes about
"the cherry hung with snow" was written by A.E. Houseman who
lived in England.

Endeavor

When my sister's Girl Scout Troop comes to our house she serves
them date bars from a recipe in *The Fanny Farmer Cookbook*. Then
she directs them in a dramatic performance of Vachel Lindsay's poem,
"The Potatoes Dance."

> *Down cellar, said the cricket,*
> *Down cellar, said the cricket,*
> *Down cellar, said the cricket,*
> *I saw a ball last night.*

The girls wear costumes made from burlap sacks my mother sewed
on her Singer. The young girls sway back and forth, dance and twirl
reciting their lines. Eyes dreamy, at one with the language and
rhythms.

When their mothers attend the performance of "The Potatoes' Dance"
they are uncomfortable with what they see. They want their daughters
completing projects; leaf collections and crocheted hot pads for
Christmas gifts. Not this creative dancing and language strange and
curiously foreign even though words they speak are in English, and
their daughters have learned them by heart.

Colonel Jasper Mint Julep

My father chose him because he was the runt. When we went to Frank
Morgan's house to choose a puppy he sat away from the others, off to
the side without moving. I named him Jasper because he's the color of
a desert jasper stone I saw in someone's rock collection. My father
added Colonel and Mint Julep.

He jumps up onto my mother's hips while she's vacuums, hops behind
her down the hall. Sometimes he mounts her while she's standing still.
She laughs when she says, "I have enough passion to satisfy the entire
French Army."

Standardized Testing

My senior year we take intelligence tests, and tests on history and math. The room's filled with desks right next to each other. Overhead the light's dark yellow. Rain against the windows.

I'm assigned a desk in the middle. We are told not to talk or look at our neighbor's test. The teacher in the front hands out test booklets and sharp pencils. We are not to open them until he says to. He will read the instructions aloud, then we may begin.

The room feels hot.

White sealed test booklet. Yellow wooden pencil. "Open it, and turn to the instructions." His voice melts to waves; they jump and dart. I hurry through without understanding the questions then hand it in. He whispers, "Time isn't up."

I run to the girls' restroom. Stay in a stall until the test is over.

When I meet the counselor to discuss college applications she tells me my score for the IQ test came back. She says, "Don't waste your time applying to colleges or universities," handing me a brochure for a Beauty School training program beginning in June, two weeks after graduation.

Cataclysm

My mother bakes brownies for my father. He'll be home from Boeing soon. Doris Day on the record player, "Day by day I'm falling more in love with you…"

She wears five strands of golden glass beads. When my father comes in he walks to where she holds the pan of brownies just out of the oven. She wears a padded mitt. He hits the pan from underneath so the brownies fly into the air before they fall onto the floor.

Mistress of Ceremonies

My mother's afraid of the ferry ride from Bainbridge Island to Seattle.
Crossing over water overwhelms, yet one day she attempts it on her
own wearing a dress she made, blue roses on polished chintz. The
short skirt shows her graceful legs and ankles.

When I return from school two strange men sit on the sofa. My
mother's smiling, looks shy. They saw her on the ferry leaning against
the railing and thought she "was hot." Something about her legs, the
way she was standing.

Her feet were probably poised, heel of her left foot resting on top of
her right one, like a ballet dancer.

They asked if she was lost. Fearing she'd encounter trouble in the city
they encouraged her to return and drove her home.

She brought them instant coffee. Thin blue cardigan tossed on the
footstool in front of the overstuffed arm chair, she's pleased to be with
these men who noticed her. I hear them laughing from my room after
excusing myself and shutting the door.

First Try

I ask my mother and father for the *Better Homes and Gardens New Cookbook* for my fifteenth birthday. Its red and white checked cover with five rings snaps open so you can add more recipes. It divides into sections with pink tabs: *Breads, Casseroles, One-dish meals, Eggs & Cheese, Meats, Poultry, Fish, Vegetables*, and *Desserts*. Sections in the back are for *Table Settings* and *Entertainment*; glass table set with frosty blue linen mats. White dishes hold circles of strawberries filled with blueberries sprinkled with powdered sugar. *The Special Meals* section explains how to plan a *Supper on the Porch* and *A Birthday Buffet* with a *Make-Your-Own Sandwich Tray*.

When I undo the ribbon and take the cookbook out of the gift-wrap my father says he's looking forward to eating the meals I'll prepare. Soon I decide to make *Tuna Bake with Cheese Swirls* for dinner. The recipe calls for green pepper, onion, a can of chicken with rice soup, milk, lemon juice, a can of tuna, then flour, milk, butter, and salt to make the light crusty biscuit pin-wheels into which you fold half a cup of grated American cheese.

I buy ingredients at the grocery store, set them on the counter with measuring spoons and cups. When everything's mixed together and topped with biscuit pin-wheels, I put the Pyrex dish in the oven to bake. At the last minute I broil the pin-wheels until they are "golden" like the recipe says.

My mother, father, and sister sit around the table. Wearing padded oven mitts I carry the baking dish into the dining room then place it on a hot pad in front of my father. We hand him our plates. He gives each of us a helping. I pass the salad made yesterday, the *Twenty-four-hour Salad* with fruit, quartered marshmallows, and whipped cream. I chilled it overnight like the cookbook said, then decorated the top with orange sections and maraschino cherries just before serving.

I look at my plate, take small bites of the *Tuna Bake*. No one speaks until my mother observes how "beautiful" everything looks and how "wonderful" the dinner is.

My father clears his throat, holds his fork filled with biscuit swirl and tuna in the air and says, "Darlin' this is the best meal I've eaten in my entire life. It's perfection. You really know how to cook. I don't know how you did it."

It's quiet for a long time. My sister keeps eating. My mother looks down at her plate. I feel I've injured my mother by making this meal for the family. I wanted it to be like the pictures in the red and white checked cookbook where everyone is having a good time. After dessert the hostess looks at her guests and says, "Shall we go into the living room?"

Homecoming

The summer I'm sixteen my father goes to Bangor, Maine for two
weeks. He's an Oral Presentations Coach at Boeing and trains
engineers to give speeches. He doesn't know what they're talking
about, but helps them anyway.

Every day he calls my mother. She loves the sound of his voice,
says how much she misses him.

The night he comes home from the airport it's late. He still has to take
the ferry to Bainbridge Island. When he comes in with his suitcase my
mother wants to fix him scrambled eggs. He says he isn't hungry.

Later I hear them. He's been drinking, says he's going to break her leg.
I jump out of bed, run down the hall into their bedroom. I'm wearing
my floor length rayon nightgown the color of tangerines. My mother
says I look very Grecian with its scoop neck and the way it ties around
my waist three times before the long ends criss-cross into a bow.

My father stands against the window in his shorts. I beat my fists
against his chest, "Don't you dare hit her." He shrugs then says,
"I didn't hurt anybody."

My mother's sobbing. I put my arms around her, smell her clean hair
she shampooed that afternoon. Her thin blue cotton nightgown's the
color of robins' eggs. I know she wants him to hold her, and for him
to smell her hair.

Mission

My father buys groceries after he comes home from work or on the weekends. When he asks my mother for her "list" it takes her time to finish it. One morning she walks to the grocery store down the path across the street from our house through yellow Scotch Broom.

She returns carrying a paper sack filled with groceries. Air of triumph, for as she walked down the aisle cans stacked high on either side almost collapsed. She saw them moving.

Menacing. Unstoppable.

Sparkplug

I dance around the house while popular songs play on KJR or KOL.
Eyelash curler between my thumb and forefinger I twirl then pause,
lean backwards until my ponytail touches the floor as I grasp the
bedroom doorway.

My mother watches, clasps her hands. I feel radiant. Light on my feet.
Singing in the rain with Gene Kelly.

After school when I call out, "Mom, I'm home," she greets me
expectant and eager for news. I tell her which boy said, "Hi," share
confusions of math, and speak of the trouble I got into for talking
in class to Ellen or Rose.

In my absence light folds into a drawer like clothes at the end of a
season. But when I return as she hangs on my every word, the house
begins to fill with alabaster clouds.

Ambience

All morning she sketches dark shapes. Shuddering birds emerge
from gray cocoon-like clouds. Her slanting pencil works insistent
strokes. Beds unmade, laundry heaped, tufts of dog hair on the rug.
Broken bamboo shade covers the glass door leading onto the deck.
Impossible to get it on the level. Tchaikovsky's *Swan Lake* plays
on the Magnavox. Scratches crackle until it's afternoon.

Psychosis: 1. The state of inhabiting a superior tone of mind where ordinary and/or limited aspects of reality are enhanced, deepened, and made more true as the result of the ability to see and comprehend via an astute uncensored perceptual energy.   2. An exquisite ability to embrace nuances of what is present but not always discerned. This may be in relation to what others say about an individual or in connection to threats and dangers a less attuned sensibility would not be able to recognize or grasp.

Mother Daughter Tea

In May of my senior year we model the outfits we made in Home Ec at the fashion show in the school auditorium. Coffee, tea, and cookies are served to our mothers. Bouquets of lilacs line the stage. Their fragrance fills the room.

I made a green and white wool suit with a fringed scarf from a Vogue Classic pattern. The jacket has three bound buttonholes and covered buttons. We enter from the wings of the stage, turn slowly; hold to the left and right before descending the stairs. A moderator says our name and describes each outfit in detail. Violin music wafts behind us.

My mother arrives wearing a suit she made from a winter coat, black and russet tweed. It looks lumpy and unfinished. Runs an inch wide in her black stockings. She smiles and waves. I want to disappear.

Once

It resided in the basement of our house in Gardner, on the floor of a
closet in a bedroom just off the basement, a room with wallpaper and
windows used to store boxes, suitcases, and my father's footlocker.

I used to open it up and sometimes trace his name in the white letters
on the top of the olive green trunk. A number in white below his name.
The footlocker said "Antwerp."

Inside his canteen. It had two dents and smelled musty. Beside it his
metal cup, bowl, and "silverware" stacked inside a canvas bag. He
called this his "Mess Kit," and carried it through the war along with
his canteen. Letters from him to my mother and from my mother to
him were in the footlocker. When I read them I could hear his voice
telling her how much he missed her and wanted to come home. He
talked about the baby he wanted to hold and how we would be a
family. She wrote to him and called him, "Darling."

When I closed the footlocker I felt as if my mother and father were
safe inside. They were young and loved each other there. I knew
I was the baby they talked about, the one I'd seen in a photograph
of the three of us when he was home on furlough and I was a few
months old.

Care Package

Girls in my sorority receive packages from home, usually cookies. Cheryl Tjossem's mother sends Nanaimo Bars packed tight in a coffee can. Each bar has four layers of chocolate and butter cream. Cheryl shares them.

One day I call my mother and ask her to send me cookies. She sounds surprised, then asks what kind. I say, "peanut butter."

When my care package arrives I open a shallow box, unfold the wax paper. The cookies are broken into small pieces and crumbs.

I eat a piece of a cookie then empty the rest into the garbage can in the kitchen. Lines on the top of the broken piece where my mother pressed the fork on the cookie dough before she put it in the oven to bake.

Landing

Calendar. I mark off days until Thanksgiving vacation.

Nine hours on the bus through wheat fields and small towns.
We arrive. Greyhound station where my father waits. He's drunk.
Eyes shiny he slurs his words as I get into the car, "Susie made
cheerleader you know. She'd tried out for Junior Varsity." He
tells me this again as though I won't remember to acknowledge it.

We take the ferry, drive home. My sister screams my name, jumps up
and down. She's wearing lipstick. Eye makeup. I see my bed through
the open door. Bare mattress. Striped ticking.

Mother's Weekend

My mother and sister take the bus to Pullman the spring of my
sophomore year. My sister is in eighth grade, and I've arranged
for them to stay overnight in my sorority house. There will be a
Dress Dinner where we sing Tri Delta songs and Song Fest where
my sorority sings "Black is the Color of My True Love's Hair"
with the Sig Eps.

Late in the evening my mother sits on the floor of the basement room
where some of us smoke. She's wearing an apricot house coat with
puffed sleeves and big buttons in a circle with a few of my sorority
sisters. She laughs with them as if she's the one going to college. I feel
far away as I watch and go to check on my sister.

At the end of Sunday Dress Dinner when everyone has left the table to
go to the Song Fest my mother still sits in her chair. I ask her why she
isn't getting up. She beckons for me to lean down so she can whisper
in my ear. She's having her period and needs a tampon.

I'm aware how helpless she is sitting there afraid the blood will run
down her leg if she walks across the pale blue carpet in the living
room. The carpet resonates with the blue of the French Drapes and
complements the crimson satin chairs. The Tri Delta House is white
with pillars around the stairs. It made me think of Tara and Scarlett
when she sat on the stairs in her hoop skirt with Brent and Stuart,
the Tarleton twins. That was before they went to war, and before
everything went up in flames and Melanie died. I think she died;
at least she suffered in a way very different from Scarlett.

Dusting Powder

My junior year in college I take Geology 101, one of four science requirements for English Majors. The first day Professor David Rahm makes a peanut butter jelly sandwich he slices in half. Then he explains how faults in the earth finally give way under thousands of years of pressure. This causes earthquakes. He holds two halves of the sandwich together, then lets one "slip." I see how faults work.

After this geology becomes more difficult, even though I memorize vocabulary and definitions enough to the pass the tests. I spend hours in the lab trying to figure out the life of rocks. On Mohs scale of mineral hardness the diamond is hardest, talc softest. I touch a white greasy lump of talc with my finger, think of the tin of *Quelque Fleur* talcum powder on my mother's dresser. Small bouquet of flowers sketched on the white container whose metal top adjusts to open or close tiny holes when I sprinkle powder onto the palm of my hand. Rubbed in it smells faintly of honeysuckle, a gift she keeps for years, powder that once was a rock.

Reprieve

I smoke Salems in the corner of the women's rest room at a wooden desk in the basement of College Hall at WSU. It's comforting, semi-dark in a rest room in the basement of the old brick building housing both Chemistry and English Departments. Smell of sulphur wafts down the stairs, fragrance of rotten eggs. I inhale, then slowly exhale, watch smoke rise up past the mirror toward the ceiling.

Sackcloth and Ashes

Ursula Luna is a mother in the pre-school co-op. She's from Germany; her husband's from Cuba. She makes spicy sauces with peppers and avocado. Ursula's tall and thin, has long hair and doesn't wear make up. Her son's name is Sasha, Russian for Alexander.

I like her precise efficient way, the spare apartment decorated with inexpensive pillows and mis-matched furniture. We take our three-year-old sons to the Green Lake playground. Sometimes we have coffee and talk about ourselves. She was a model in Germany before she met her husband. She's homesick. Both our husbands are busy with graduate school.

One day Ursula tells me I apologize all the time. I don't know what she's talking about. She says I say, "I'm sorry," when I didn't do anything wrong.

After this I began to hear myself but keep apologizing as though I've caused irreparable damage. I'm swamped with remorse, yet I haven't hit anyone or hurt my child. Even so, I'm sorry and say so, over and over and over again.

V1

no more reaching across the white field

Joan Bradford 84 years old
Green Lake, Seattle, Washington
Photo by Gary Grenell

Schoolma'am to Actress
New York Herald Tribune   *July 27,1941*

*Just a little over a year ago Joan Stone was correcting copy books
in a school in Plumber, Pa., pointing out that "cat" invariably was
spelled with a "c" and that 3 always went into 21 exactly seven times
– and now she is playing the ingénue lead in* Life with Father *which
has been resident at the Empire for twenty-one months. That's quite a
jump, and this is the way she made it.*

*While she was teaching at Plumer, Miss Stone passed as much of
her spare time as she could with a little-theatre group in Franklin –
and by June of 1940 she decided she had enough money saved (and
enough of a smattering of theatrical experience) to take a course
at Cape May, N.J. The end of that summer found her playing the
Betty Field role in* What a Life, *and into the audience one evening,
complete with walking stick and dead pan, strolled George Jean
Nathan.*

*Nathan is considered as caustic and severe a critic as ever harpooned
an actress—nevertheless, he was so taken with Miss Stone's performance that he went back to New York to induce Richard Watts Jr, of
the* New York Herald Tribune, *to go down to Cape May with him later
in the week.*

*Watts too came, saw, and was conquered, and when Miss Stone took
a train for New York after the engagement of* What a Life, *two drama
critics were sitting at her side, giving her tips on how to crash Broadway.*

*Miss Stone followed the leads and found herself playing opposite
Taylor Holmes in a road company of* The Man Who Came to Dinner.
*After six weeks she was back in New York, and, as ingénues have to
eat, she took a typing and filing job in the* "Information Please" *office.
Last May she read the role of Mary Skinner for Howard Lindsay, and
then, five weeks ago, just as she was beginning to give up hope, she
was engaged.*

*Incidentally, the role of Mary already has proved to be something of
a springboard for two young actresses. Theresa Wright, the original*

133

"girl who had never met a Yale man before," left Life with Father *to go out to Hollywood to play Bette Davis's daughter in* The Little Foxes. *Stone won't be doing any springing for quite a while, however—she's in it for the duration.*

NEW YORK HERALD TRIBU

Joan Stone of "Life With Father"

Schoolma'am to Actress

JUST a little over a year ago Joan Stone was correcting copy books in a school in Plumer, Pa., pointing out that "cat" invariably was spelled with a "c" and that 3 always went into 21 exactly seven times—and now she is playing the ingenue lead in "Life With Father," which has been resident at the Empire for twenty-one months. That's quite a jump, and this is the way she made it:

While she was teaching at Plumer, Miss Stone passed as much of her spare time as she could with a little-theater group in Franklin—and by June of 1940 she decided she had enough money saved (and enough of a smattering of theatrical experience) to take a course at Cape May, N. J. The end of that summer found her playing the Betty Field role in "What a Life," and into the audience one evening, complete with walking stick and dead pan, strolled George Jean Nathan.

Nathan is considered as caustic and severe a critic as ever harpooned an actress—nevertheless, he was so taken with Miss Stone's performance that he went back to New York to induce Richard Watts jr., of the New York Herald Tribune, to go down to Cape May with him later in the week.

Watts, too, came, saw and was conquered, and when Miss Stone took a train for New York after the engagement of "What a Life," two drama critics were sitting at her side, giving her tips on how to crash Broadway.

Miss Stone followed the leads and found herself playing opposite Taylor Holmes in a road company of "The Man Who Came to Dinner." After six weeks she was back in New York, and, as ingenues have to eat, she took a typing and filing job in the "Information, Please" office. Last may she read the role of Mary Skinner for Howard Lindsay, and then, five weeks ago, just as she was beginning to give up hope, she was engaged.

Incidentally, the role of Mary already has proved to be something of a springboard for two young actresses. Theresa Wright, the original "girl who had never met a Yale man before," left "Life With Father" to go out to Hollywood to play Bette Davis's daughter in "The Little Foxes," and Katharine Bard, who replaced her, now is playing ingenue leads at the Bass Rocks Theater. Ms. Miss Stone won't be doing any springing for quite a while, however—she's in it for the duration.

New York Herald Tribune
Reproduced by permission of the
International New York Times.

134

Vandamm

A scene of "Life With Father," the young man being John Drew Devereaux, the very pretty girl, Joan Stone.

New York Times January 11, 1942

For Joan Stone*, tomato eater,
pineapple-ring addict, stuffed crab
fan, oyster-trier and coincidental
pace-maker, milk-sherry-Planter's
Punch-mint julep-Cutty Sark inebriate,
chocolate soda enthusiast, big cherry à la
maraschino fiend, Upham bread
gobbler, and adventuress generally,

With the lifted eyebrows of
her old boy-friend,

Lee Shubert.

* Alias Jane St. Clair, Jessie Stein and
Jeanne Szvrntzswicki.

George Jean Nathan inscribed the name "Lee Shubert" in
Murder without Makeup, a gift to Joan set in a theatre where
death strikes on the most fashionable opening night of the season.

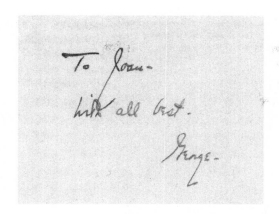

Book inscription to *Encyclopedia of the
Theatre* by George Jean Nathan from George
Jean Nathan to Joan New York 1942

Inscriptions by George Jean Nathan in two books he gave to my
mother:

For Joan Stone, tomato eater, pineapple-ring addict, stuffed crab fan,
oyster-trier and coincidental face-maker, milk – sherry - Planter's
Punch – mint julep – Cutty Sark inebriate, chocolate soda enthusiast,
big cherry 'a la maraschino fiend, Uphaus bread gobbler, and
adventuress generally,*

> *With the lifted eyebrow of
> her old boy-friend,
> Lee Shubert.*

**Alias Jane St. Clair, Jessie Stein and
Jeannie Szventzswiski*

*

*To Joan –
    With all best .
        George -*

Encyclopedia of the Theatre   by George Jean Nathan
Alfred A. Knopf New York 1940

To Be Married On Sunday

BENJAMIN BRADFORD, son of Dr. and Mrs. Arthur Howe Bradford, and his fiancee, Miss Joan Thomas Stone, daughter of Mrs. Joseph William Stone of Franklin, Pa. The couple will be married Sunday at the Central Congregational Church where the bridegroom-elect's father is pastor. Dr. Bradford will officiate at the ceremony. The bride is a member of the cast of "Life With Father," now playing in New York. Mr. Bradford is a member of the staff of the New York Times. He was graduated from Brown University with the class of 1940. Miss Stone is a graduate of Indiana State Teachers' College in Pennsylvania.

A WOMAN'S PHILOSOPHY

"To Be Married on Sunday" The *Providence Journal*,
January 4, 1942.

Jan. 8th 1942

Dear Mrs. Bradford:

We wish very much indeed that we could be present at the marriage of Joan to your son. Unfortunately we had previous commitments, one of which was an anniversary party which of course fell upon the particular day and date.

My husband and I are so very happy about the marriage of Joan and Ben. Joan is one of the most sweet and untouched girls that it has ever been our good fortune to meet in the theatre. The part that Joan plays in our play is that of a young and unsophisticated girl, just on the threshold of life, and Joan is so completely that in herself that it made her an excellent choice. And because she is so completely that we have come to love and admire her very much.

I think we met your son before he had even met Joan as he came to our house to interview my husband and wrote a splendid article from this interview for his paper. We took an immediate liking to him and having since seen more of him when he has called for Joan at the theatre, our first good impression of him deepens with each meeting. All of this has given us a sure conviction of the rightness of this marriage.

We have always felt there was a blessing on LIFE WITH FATHER .. that it had its own particular Guardian Angel. That it brought Joan and Ben together is part of the blessing.

Please forgive my use of the typewriter, but my handwriting is so bad you could never forgive it.

Cordially
Dorothy Stickney Lindsay

Letter from Dorothy Stickney Lindsay who played Vinnie, the mother,
in *Life with Father,* the longest running non-musical play on Broadway, written
by her husband, Howard Lindsay

Stranded

My mother doesn't drive. She drove when she was young and went
to Normal School and when she taught in a one room schoolhouse for
two years. I imagine a black car on country roads, cloud of dust until
it disappears.

One day she starts the car. Her left arm sticks out the window. Her
hand trembles. She's tries to give a turn signal and cannot control
her hand or make it stop. Her arm looks feeble, helpless, her hand
a terrified bird. Slowly the car moves up to the road then stops. She
gets out, slams the door, walks into the house.

Slip Up

The slipping tries to walk then slides, glass mountain princes cannot scale to reach the princess. It recedes like the tide pulling back and back, froth on the waves. I wave good-by, get used to the slipping or think I do. Once more she talks of the white eyelet shirtdress she'll sew and wear with a belt. Tam dipping over one eye when my father courted her in Greenwich Village. Liverwurst sandwiches in their apartment before I was born. I see them laughing, black velvet beret. She never makes the shirtdress. Today the teacher in a floral cotton dress stands before her class, pencil behind her ear. She draws our names on flowers, bright paper pinned to the corkboard. But the slipping starts just as I've gained momentum enough to carry the bolt of cotton eyelet up to the counter where the woman will roll it open to cut what I need. "How much?" she will ask. Yardage. The pattern lies in the drawer of the house that disappears at a moment like this. Nowhere exactitude. The slipping sneaks beneath my feet. Lights dim on the other side of the wall. "Never mind," I say. The woman sighs. I've let her down again.

Ex Cathedra

Once my mother took the bus by herself. When she returned she told my sister and me how she paused to check if she had the exact change for the fare in her black coin purse. She showed us how she'd opened the gold clasp before getting on the bus. Her intense recounting caused us to roll our eyes.

Hurt on her face she stopped mid-sentence. Her eyes became the sky. We'd injured something beyond us, crucified a conduit to the cosmos. We learned to take her seriously. Not to question. Listen as if to an oracle's delivered truth.

Episode

On mattress ticking in a pale yellow nightgown. Three days. Will
not move. Nothing moves. On the floor cuckoo clocks tell time. High
noon. The river rises. What's the full moon doing up there like a bad
balloon. August. Rip tides. Undercurrents sweep us away.

I'm thirty-two. My mother's fifty-six. I drive her to the state mental
hospital at Steilacoom.

Shock treatments. Mellaril, Thorazine, Haldol. For years a waxen
face that never smiles. She cannot lift a foot or raise her arm. Gone the
eyes she turned to the ceiling counting each hole in the squares.

Artiste

After she stops her medication, after her cataract surgery, my mother returns to drawing. Rises at 3:00 am. Soon hundreds of angular girls or women, winsome animals, birds, and flowers appear. She sketches on brown paper bags, paper towels, backs of paper placemats, backs of envelopes, on tablets and other surfaces. She creates multimedia collages using pastels, water colors, colored pencils, and crayons.

One day she takes the bus to Pioneer Square with her art in a tablecloth. Glenn Allen of the Metropolitan Art Gallery says, "Joan, you are an artist." She will have three shows there.

Admirers will sit at her feet at the Openings as she speaks of her art, how anyone can do it, they only need to be open. They only need to let it out. She will talk of how her art grew out of her suffering, how it is the child within.

One of her sketches will sell for $1000. She will say a doctor wants to take her photograph.

Sprite

My father describes his first impression of my mother:

I liked her immediately. She was not tall but her body was slim and graceful. Her eyes made a tremendous impression on me for they were wide apart, seemed large and luminous as they sparkled with merriment. Her blonde hair was cut in the page boy style. She was wearing a Tyrolean blouse with colorful suspenders matching her skirt. There was something extremely theatrical about her, but she also had the appearance of a young girl in her teens.

On the cross-town bus heading for the subway to take me to the Village I found myself thinking about Joan Stone – the word "sprite" came to mind as I responded to my feelings for her. I loved her merriment, her piquancy and her simplicity. She seemed full of life but also vulnerable – as if her feelings could be easily crushed. I sensed she was sensitive and emotional though her merriment seemed real – not a façade.

*

Hemingway touched a curl on her cheek at the Algonquin Hotel at 59 W 44th St in Manhattan. He said she was pretty. She danced with a boy in the gazebo summer evenings in Franklin, Pennsylvania, light brown hair down to her shoulders.

When I bring my fiancé home from college she enters the living room eager and breathless. He thinks she's my sister, six years younger than I am. She looks as if he asked her to dance. She's all eyes.

*

When she's eighty-six she stops walking and grows frail. After six weeks I call 911. The ambulance takes her to the hospital. Lying on the upright table in the ER she says proudly, "I'm the filthiest patient they've ever seen." She's been scrubbed, cleaned up, hair no longer matted. They cut out the clumps, combed the gray wisps to frame her face in tendrils. Smiling a toothless smile she raises her thin arms to talk with her hands as always, tells the male nurse how "sweet" he is. Arms curve as she moves, eyes intense and bright. Her captive audience seems charmed as much as they must have been amazed.

145

August

We walk across a field. Grasses high where insects buzz and sing,
russet Indian Paintbrush near goldenrod and Queen Anne's lace.
Mrs. Cowdrey walks slowly toward us. In each hand she carries an
orange. Her white apron falls all the way to the ground. She holds
it up to keep from tripping. When we meet in the middle of the field
she hands one orange to me, one to my mother. For many years after
my mother will say how when I was only three I said, "Here comes
Old Mrs. Cowdrey walking across the field in her draggy down
apron."

Of the Girl I'm Taking to the Easter Parade

Where in the world did you get that red patent leather chapeau with grosgrain ribbon trialing down the back and two white plumes glued to the brim for the Easter parade passing down Fifth Avenue with drums and women in spiked red patent leather heels twirling batons as they hum "In Your Easter Bonnet" or "Here Comes Peter Cotton Tail" around abandoned floats filled up with gigantic yellow chicks and baskets overflowing with jillions of purple, green, orange, pink, and white coconut jelly beans rolling onto the sidewalk no one thinks to leave because of anticipation's white gloves and purses with the perfect click whispering old promises new with every spring?

Final Curtain

Rooms grow smaller. Walls close in. Light recedes when I visit.
No clear surface to set down a teacup.

Once we walked down the street in Point Lookout, Long Island. I am
five and wear the yellow frock she made; puffed sleeves and sash in
dotted Swiss, handstitched tucks across the bodice. On my feet white
anklets, patent leather mary janes, silver buckles for the shiny black
straps. She's donned a flowered print dress and straw hat with a brim,
spectator pumps in white and brown.

I hold her hand while the Good Humor man drives past ringing his bell.
He stops. She buys two chocolate covered ice cream bars wrapped in
paper on wooden sticks. We sit on the church steps to eat them.

She is pretty, not worried or strange. Light on the steps falls around us.

Snowflake

She breathed. And then she didn't.

Twilight

I ride the Ferris wheel in a seat for two. The man locks the pole in place so I won't fall out. It moves in short jerks because it stops to let another person on. Most seats hold two people. I clutch the pole across my lap with both hands, rock back and forth when the Ferris wheel stops. A long line waits to get on. Soon I'm at the top looking down at people and rides below. I see my mother and father. My mother holds my sister's hand. She's too young to go on the Ferris wheel. The music starts up. Now the wheel's turning around and around. I feel the wind when we go down; my stomach sinks. When I rise to the top I see my mother and father waving. They look like two tiny toy people. I cannot see their faces. My mother's long coat almost touches the ground. My father wears his hat with a brim. I could hold them in my hand. We could start all over again and I would carry them.

Furlough

Ben home on furlough during World War II with Joan and Joanie
Providence, Rhode Island November 1943

About the Author

Joan Fiset is a therapist and teacher. *Now the Day is Over* (Blue Begonia 1997) won the King County Publication Award. Her poems have appeared in *Trickhouse*, *Tarpaulin Sky*, the *Seattle Review* and others. She lives in Seattle with her husband, Louis.